ANIMAL PREDATORS

Leopard Seals

SANDRA MARKLE

Lerner Publications Company / Minneapolis

The Animal World is Full of
PREDATORS.

Predators are the hunters that find, catch, and eat other animals—their prey—in order to survive. Every environment has its chain of hunters. The smaller, slower, less able predators become prey for the bigger, faster, more cunning hunters. And everywhere, there are just a few kinds of predators at the top of the food chain. *In Antarctica, one of these is the leopard seal.*

Leopard seals spend their lives hunting in the frigid waters of the Southern Ocean surrounding Antarctica. They have a thick layer of blubber, or fat, beneath their skin. This blubber protects them from the cold and traps their body heat. They can easily float on the water's surface because the fat layer is lighter than solid muscle. Sometimes leopard seals hunt by just floating and watching for prey. Their big eyes see well in the dim underwater world. Their spotted coat is dark gray on their heads and backs and lighter, silvery gray below, on their stomachs. It helps them blend in with the changing shadows beneath the waves.

Sometimes leopard seals hide in the pack ice and watch for a chance to ambush prey. Pack ice is made of floating, drifting pieces of ice. It forms when the wintertime ocean ice crust breaks up. This hiding place lasts into December, midsummer in Antarctica.

Other times leopard seals swim in search of prey. This leopard seal saw an Antarctic fur seal pup playing in the shallows. It ambushed this prey by surging ashore with the waves. Then it grabbed the pup.

Sometimes leopard seals hunt underwater. This lets them stay hidden while they swim close to their prey. The seals can hold their breath for about ten minutes before they need to surface.

When they surface to take a breath, they look around, watching for Adelie penguins and other prey. The Adelies rest and raise their young out of the water. When a female leopard seal discovers a group of Adelies like these, she stays close and waits.

Krill

The Adelies are predators too. They feed on small, shrimplike krill and fish. To find food, they have to leave land and dive into the ocean. Before they do, the hungry Adelies pile up at the ice edge. Finally, one dives in and the rest quickly follow. The penguins find safety by entering the sea in a group. They stay close together at first and then spread out to hunt.

The female leopard seal ignores the group of Adelies. She focuses instead on a lone penguin crossing a patch of thin ice. Seeing the hunter, the penguin dives in and flaps its paddlelike wings to fly through the water. The female leopard seal dives and chases after the penguin.

The female seal holds her hind flippers close together like a fin. She sweeps her torpedo-shaped body from side to side and races in pursuit of her prey. The seal steers with her long front flippers and then strokes with them for a burst of speed. Hunter and prey swim for their lives.

The leopard seal bites. The penguin twists just in time. The seal's big canine teeth only graze the Adelie. Before the predator can bite again, the penguin reaches the ice edge and jumps out of the water. The female leopard seal follows. She is a big predator. She weighs nearly 800 pounds (363 kilograms). She is 10 feet (2.9 meters) long. But she can only hump along like a caterpillar on land. She quickly falls behind the injured penguin. The other Adelies stay out of reach of the leopard seal's big jaws.

The injured penguin waddles away from the sea edge. It is safe among the thousands of other Adelies raising their chicks. The leopard seal gives up the chase and returns to the sea. Adelie and chinstrap penguins are all nesting close together. There are plenty of other prey available in the sea, her natural hunting ground.

Besides being able to see well, the female leopard seal has a keen sense of hearing. She has no ears you can see. She receives sound right through the bones of her head. The sound travels from the bones to her inner ear. This is the way she recognizes and tracks the sounds of prey and the voices of other leopard seals.

Moving her head from side to side, the female seal homes in on the sound of one chinstrap penguin. She dives, blowing air out in a burst of bubbles. Breathing out nearly empties her lungs of air. This helps keep her underwater when she dives. Her slitlike nostrils snap shut to keep water out of her lungs as she launches her attack.

Moving nearly silently, the leopard seal sneaks up on her prey. As she gets close, she opens her jaws wide, ready to bite. At the same instant, she lifts her tongue. She also lowers her soft palate, the muscles at the back of her mouth. These actions keep water from flooding down her throat.

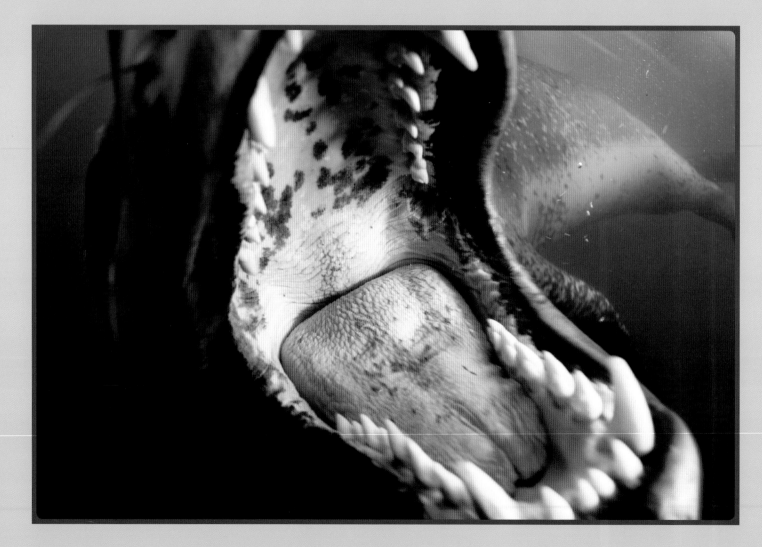

She strikes with a mouthful of strong, pointed teeth. They are perfect for stabbing and holding onto slippery prey. Her biggest weapons, her canine teeth, are nearly 1 inch (2.5 centimeters) long. She bites to make the kill.

The female leopard seal carries her prey to the surface. There, holding it locked in her jaws, she jerks her head from side to side. Since leopard seals lack molars, the teeth that grind and chew, the female has to shake the carcass to rip the tough skin and get to the meat.

She then dives underwater again to eat. She tears chunks of meat off the bones and gulps them down. A flap of tissue in her throat prevents water from going into her lungs as she swallows underwater. When she's eaten most of the flesh, she lets go of what's left of the penguin's body.

The remains of her meal drift down to the sea stars and other scavengers waiting on the ocean floor. Swimming away, the female leopard seal starts hunting again. Prey is so plentiful, she easily catches and eats three more penguins. When she grabs one more chinstrap penguin, she plays with it the way a cat toys with a mouse. She tosses it into the air and chases after it again and again. Finally, when the penguin swims away with a burst of speed, she lets it escape.

The female leopard seal hauls out onto an ice floe, a raftlike chunk of ice. There, she stretches out to rest and then sleep in the bright glow of daylight. The sun never sets during the Antarctic summer.

While the female leopard seal sleeps, the ice drifts. When she wakes up, she has to swim back to the area in which she usually hunts. On the way, her whiskers, called vibrissae, help her detect prey moving in the water. She tracks down several fish before catching a penguin. The penguin will be her last meal for a while.

Soon after the female leopard seal hauls out onto the ice again, she gives birth to a pup—a male. The pup is a big baby. He is about 5 feet (1.5 m) long and weighs almost 60 pounds (27 kg). The pup is born with almost no blubber. He has a coat of thick, long hair to keep him warm. He nuzzles along his mother's belly to find a nipple. Then he suckles, feeding on the milk she produces.

For the next month, the female leopard seal won't go off to hunt. There is little chance that predators, like killer whales, will find the pup. But the female doesn't want to risk losing track of him in the maze of ice floating on the Southern Ocean. She'll stay with her pup, resting on the ice or swimming nearby. Her body will draw the energy it needs from her blubber to stay warm, be active, and produce milk for her baby.

The leopard seal pup nurses often on his mother's rich milk—milk much creamier than cow's milk. He quickly grows bigger and fatter and develops a thick layer of blubber. And because he will soon have to catch prey to feed himself, his first teeth are adult teeth.

When he's just three weeks old, he begins to molt. He sheds his thick baby coat and grows adult fur. About this time, his mother rolls over onto her belly each time he tries to suckle. This prevents him from nursing. By the time he is about a month old, she will swim away from him forever. She leaves him hungry, and it isn't long before he starts hunting.

At first, the young leopard seal mainly eats fish and krill because these are easy to catch. After he scoops up a mouthful of water and krill, he uses his tongue to push the water out of his mouth through the spaces between his teeth. Then he swallows the krill that are left.

If he can catch them, he'll also eat bigger prey, such as penguins. At the same time the female leopard seal left her pup to fend for himself, parent penguins head out to sea to feed and fatten up before winter. The young penguins left behind become so hungry they dive into the ocean to go hunting for the first time. This gives the young male leopard seal lots of prey to catch. The young penguins are as new to avoiding predators as he is to hunting. He has lots of chances to practice hunting and soon learns how to catch a meal.

Meanwhile, the female leopard seal is ready to mate again. She is only ready for about three days, so she needs to locate a mate quickly. This is not easy when males and females live and hunt alone over the vast Southern Ocean. The female calls out long hoots and trills. The sounds she makes are all deep, low tones that may carry as far as 25 miles (40 kilometers). She repeats the same group of sounds over and over, like a song with an endlessly repeating chorus.

Male leopard seals sing too. In fact, they've been singing their songs many hours each day since October. That's because different female leopard seals become ready to mate at different times from October through January.

Two male leopard seals answer this female's calls. They swim around and sing at each other, holding their mouths open wide to show their teeth. Finally, one gives up and swims away. The winning male approaches the female. They sing to each other too before they mate.

As the days grow much shorter and colder, the puzzle pieces of pack ice freeze together again. The penguins head north, where large areas of water remain open and krill are more plentiful. The young male leopard seal follows. He needs to find lots of prey to make up for being a hunter in training. If his attempt to catch a penguin fails, he is likely to be able to catch fish or squid or krill to fill his empty belly.

The female leopard seal stays behind and keeps on hunting in her usual area. With the penguins leaving, she looks for other prey, such as fish and young crabeater seals. Until the sea ice becomes winter thick, she only has to butt her head against this icy crust to break through to take a breath.

When the ice crust becomes too thick to push through, it cracks, creating riverlike channels. The female leopard seal hunts along these channels, making trips under the ice between breaths. She senses fish and other prey with her vibrissae before she sees them in the dim waters under the ice. Sometimes she meets up with a cloud of plankton, tiny plants and animals. She swims into this cloud to catch mouthfuls of small prey.

Although she mated and became pregnant in February, her baby doesn't start to develop for about two months. Then it will continue to grow for nine more months. This delay means the leopard seal pup will be born during Antarctica's summer. By then the penguins will have returned to breed and raise their chicks. The female leopard seal will have lots of prey to hunt. She'll be able to rebuild her blubber before she stops hunting to care for her pup.

Then the cycle continues. The female's new pup, a female, will be on her own just as the penguin chicks and crabeater seal pups are entering the sea. There will be plenty of prey for a new generation of leopard seals on the hunt.

Looking Back

- Take another look at page 11. How does a leopard seal's body shape help it swim fast?

- Check out the seal on the ice on page 12. How does the seal's body shape keep it from moving fast out of the water?

- Look back through the book's photos. How does the leopard seal's coat help it hide in plain sight and sneak up on its prey?

- Look again at the leopard seals on the cover and on page 21. What is the leopard seal able to do to its nostrils when it dives underwater? Why do you think it helps the seal to be able to do this? If you need a clue, look back to page 14.

Glossary

AMBUSH: lie in wait to attack; to make a surprise attack

BLUBBER: thick layer of fat under the skin

CANINE TEETH: cone-shaped, strong, pointed teeth on either side of the front teeth. These are a leopard seal's longest teeth, and they are used for puncturing and tearing flesh.

CARCASS: the body of a dead animal

ICE FLOE: a large, flat, raftlike chunk of floating ice

MOLT: to shed part or all of a coat or outer covering

NURSE: to feed on milk from the mother's body

PACK ICE: mix of small and large chunks of frozen seawater, floating close together. It forms when a frozen ice mass is broken up by strong waves.

PLANKTON: a collection of tiny plants and animals, drifting in the sea

PREDATOR: an animal that hunts and kills other animals in order to live

PREY: an animal that a predator catches to eat

SCAVENGER: an animal that feeds on dead animals

VIBRISSAE: sensitive facial whiskers

Further Information

Books

Hodge, Judith, and Judith Walker-Hodge. *Seals, Sea Lions, and Walruses.* Hauppauge, NY: Barron's, 1999. Compare leopard seals to their cousins: other seals, sea lions, and walruses.

McMillan, Bruce. *Summer Ice: Life Along the Antarctic Peninsula.* Boston: Walter Lorraine Books, 1995. Explore leopard seals and the other animals in their food web.

Stone, Lynn M. *Penguins.* Minneapolis: Lerner Publications Company, 2003. Learn about the many kinds of penguins that live in the Southern Ocean.

Websites

Penguins, Leopard Seal Face Off
http://news.nationalgeographic.com/news/2006/11/061113-penguins-video.html
Watch as a leopard seal hunts penguins in the sea and on the ice.

Seal Conservation Society
http://www.pinnipeds.org/species/species.htm
This is a great site for investigating and comparing different kinds of seals. Click on photos to discover facts and see more pictures.

Virtual World: Antarctica
http://www.nationalgeographic.com/crittercam/antarctica/index.html
Scientists have attached a camera to a leopard seal to catch a glimpse of where this animal travels and observe its behavior.

Index

For Dominic and Callum and their parents Paul and Katrina Knill

The author would like to thank the following people for sharing their expertise and enthusiasm: Dr. John Bengtson and Dr. Peter L. Boveng, NOAA National Marine Mammal Laboratory; Dr. Sophie Hall-Aspland, University of Sydney; and Dr. Tracey Rogers, Australian Marine Mammal Research Center. The author would also like to express a special thank-you to Skip Jeffery for his help and support during the creative process.

Photo Acknowledgments

The images in this book are used with the permission of: © Yva Momatiuk & John Eastcott/ Minden Pictures, p. 1; © Paul Nicklen/ National Geographic/Getty Images, pp. 3, 5, 11, 16, 17, 18, 19, 21, 23, 25, 27, 37; © OSF/ Doug Allan/Animals Animals, p. 6; NOAA photo by Michael K. Schwartz, p. 7; © Suzi Eszterhas/Minden Pictures, p. 8; © Skip Jeffery Photography, p. 9; © Flip Nicklin/ Minden Pictures, p. 9 (inset); © Frank Todd/Arcticphoto.com, pp. 10, 34; © Gerald L. Kooyman/Animals Animals, p. 12; © Ingrid Visser/ SeaPics.com, p. 13; © Bill Curtsinger/ National Geographic Image Collection, pp. 15, 35; © T.J. Rich/naturepl.com, p. 22; © Rick Price/Photolibrary/Getty Images, p. 24; © DWH Walton/ British Antarctic Survey, p. 26; © Doug Allan/naturepl.com, p. 29; © Rinie Van Meurs/Minden Pictures, p. 30; © Sue Flood/ The Image Bank/Getty Images, p. 31; © Paul Nicklen/ National Geographic Image Collection, p. 33.
Cover: © Paul Nicklen/ National Geographic/Getty Images.

Lerner Publications Company
A division of Lerner Publishing Group, Inc.
241 First Avenue North
Minneapolis, MN 55401 U.S.A.

Website address: www.lernerbooks.com

Websites listed in Further Reading are current at time of publication

Library of Congress Cataloging-in-Publication Data

Markle, Sandra.
    Leopard seals / by Sandra Markle.
        p.   cm. — (Animal predators)
    Includes bibliographical references and index.
    ISBN 978—1—58013—540—5 (lib. bdg. : alk. paper)
    1. Leopard seal—Juvenile literature. I. Title.
QL737.P64M33 2010
599.79'6—dc22   2008038094

Manufactured in the United States of America
1 2 3 4 5 6 — DP — 15 14 13 12 11 10